MY LITTLE BOOK OF BIG FREEDOMS

ILLUSTRATED BY CHRIS RIDDELL

Penguin Workshop
An Imprint of Penguin Random House

 IN ASSOCIATION WITH AMNESTY INTERNATIONAL

I WANT TO DRAW EVERY DAY AND PROMOTE DRAWING FOR ALL ~

Chris Riddell.

W e all want a good life, to have fun, to be safe and happy and fulfilled.

For this to happen, we need to look after one another.

In this book there are sixteen different freedoms that help us do that. They are truly wonderful, precious things.

These freedoms were created to protect us, forever.

We need to stand up for them and look after them just as they look after us.

I've drawn some pictures for you. Each of them shows one of our freedoms. I hope you like them.

Chris Riddell.

We all have the right to live.

Nobody has the right to
hurt or torture us.

Nobody has the right to
make us a slave—we cannot
make anyone else a slave
or force them to work for us.

No one has the right to imprison us without a good reason. They have to tell us that reason and let us say why we should be set free.

If we are put on trial, we must be treated fairly. Nobody can blame us for doing something bad until it is proved. The people who try us must not let anyone else tell them what to do.

You can't be punished for doing something wrong if there was no law against it when you did it.

We have the right to live with our family and live our lives in the way we choose. The government must respect our privacy.

We all have the right to think or believe in whatever we like, to have a religion, and to show it.

THOUGHT

We all have the right to the information we need to make up our own minds. We have the right to say what we think and share ideas with other people.

We all have the right
to spend time with other
people, to get together, and
to look after one another.

Every grown-up has the right to marry and have a family if they want to.

We all have the same rights. No one can take them away or give us different ones because of who we are or because we are different from them.

OWNERSHIP

Everybody has the right to own and share things. Nobody should take our things away without a good reason.

KNOWLEDGE

We all have the right
to learn.

We all have the right to take part in running our country. Every grown-up should be allowed to say who they want to be their leader.

No one is allowed to end
our lives, even if we did
something very bad.

Why this little book is important

The words and pictures in this book are about human rights. Human rights are freedoms that we are all entitled to. We may not have our own lion to guard us, or Pegasus to wrap its wings around us, but these rights are guaranteed to all of us, children and grown-ups, just because we are human. This book shows us why our human rights are so important. They help to keep us safe. Every day.

The Universal Declaration of Human Rights (UDHR) was adopted by the United Nations General Assembly on December 10, 1948, after the world's experience of World War II. When that war ended, the international community vowed to never let the atrocities that occurred during that conflict happen again. World leaders decided to create a document that would guarantee the rights of every individual everywhere. Eleanor Roosevelt, widow of President Franklin D. Roosevelt, chaired the committee that created the document. This document became the Universal Declaration of Human Rights. And the book you have just read, *My Little Book of Big Freedoms*, is inspired by the UDHR.